HYDROGEN SLEEP AND SPEED

A Verse Tale of Egypt, Rommel, Angry Gods, Caligari & Amphetamine

TH. METZGER

The Poet's Press

PITTSBURGH, PA

This is the 192nd publication of
THE POET'S PRESS
2209 Murray Avenue #3
Pittsburgh, PA 15217
www.poetspress.org

This book is also published as an Adobe Acrobat
ebook in PDF format.

ISBN 0-922558-57-4

PART I:
THE SALT
AXIS

We use not words —
but sounds full of energy.

— Corpus Hermeticum XVI

1

Only tongues and shovels
only spells and smells
only Albion's finger bones, his skull
his shoulder blades and splayed ribs
his thigh bones hollowed out
to make two trumpets
to wake the dead.

Only a fragment of polished glass
lowered on a string,
down to the tumble of brother bones.
Torchlight catches on the bright shard surface
and flares
breathed into life by the breath of the grave
by Albion's cold clay, decaying
into volatile fractions.

His brother, the Prophet Joseph Smith,
the troubler of the dead
— whom only gold and bones can satisfy —
this troubler climbs down
to brush away coffin earth and
pluck back the winding sheet.

His brother cinches tight the ropes
and a chain to draw fair Albion
from his too short earthly sleep.
As the body is lifted from its crumbling bed,
there appear guardian reptiles:
writhing beasts white as moonlight on snow
white unto lunar blueness.
Salamanders and airy specters,
water snakes and blind earthworms,
all gathered in that one shadowy dighole.

<7>

Fiery torches above and radiant reptiles below.
A wound in the earth.
A seep of ground water
which he, Prophet and Raiser of the Dead,
kneels to lap like a catamount laps the blood
of his prey.
And sucks in the exhalation of darker air —
an expelled vapor —
dead brother breathing again.

There at Brother Albion's heavenly hole,
in his holy heaves,
the endless parade of spectral history begins:
unrolling as a glowing scroll.
The prophet sees, knows, believes,
reads the future.
Lost races, lost battles, lost minds.
Lost treasure
found, hidden and lost again.
The murk of storms
and rain-bloated rivers
blood oaths
signed affidavits
proclamations
curses, blessings
revelations from God on high
half a hundred wives
and the rage of the final gun-mob.
Bullets, blood and a second
secret burial place.

<8>

2

Albion died by poison
given him by his family.
With this, no one —
neither truest believer
nor bitterest heretic —
has ever argued.
Death by calomel
by mercurous chloride
by white powder
by purgative, cathartic
found in nature, raw,
found in the form
of horn mercury.

Albion died
poisoned by his family
writhing
in the outhouse
that his bowels
might be pure
expunged of all taint
empty of sin.

Albion died at the age
of twenty-five
the good son, older brother
who built the Smith home
who worked and scrimped
who saved the family from poverty.

<9>

Albion died
yet he was dragged back
to the world of the living, revealing
to his younger brother Joseph,
and thus to the entire world,
the gods' new plan:
restoration of true religion and
redemption of the dead.

3

TO THE PUBLIC:

Whereas reports have been industriously put
        in circulation
that my son, Alvin [sic], has been removed from the place
of his interment and dissected;
which reports every person possessed
of human sensibility
must know are peculiarly calculated
to harrow up the mind of a parent
and deeply wound the feelings of relations,
I, with some of my neighbors this morning,
repaired to the grave, and removing the earth,
found the body, which had not been disturbed.

This method is taken for the purpose
of satisfying the minds of those
who have put it in circulation,
that it is earnestly requested that
they would desist therefrom.
And that it is believed by some
that they have been stimulated
more by desire to injure the reputation
of certain persons than by a philanthropy
for the peace and welfare of myself and friends.

                                        (signed)
                            Joseph Smith, Senior
                Wayne Sentinel — September 25, 1824

<11>

4

Here, all geography is sacred.
Water, land and sky
reflect the faces,
the souls and desires,
the great plan
of the gods.

Here, a river runs due north —
called by the prophet
the Nile of America:
flood-mad in springtime
overflowing its banks with
fertile black mud, indolent
the rest of the year.

Here, countless knolls,
elongated ovals of glacial drift
called drumlins
by the Irish canal diggers
who mucked their way
through Wayne County,
are scattered.
Half-submerged whale-shapes
in the green ocean of farmland,
a denser herd than anywhere else on earth.

Here, the prophet saw
long-lost Indian burial mounds.
Some drumlins were indeed opened
and inside grave-breakers found piles
of bones, teeth and weapons.

<12>

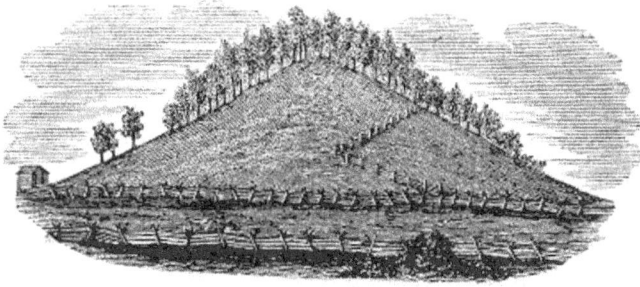

So then, why shouldn't he deem
them holy hills instead of
mere backslough of glaciers?
If all is sacred,
why shouldn't he see
with the prophetic eye
an entire civilization
fighting its last battle on the hill
he called Cumorah?
Why shouldn't he tell the story
of the greatest battle of all time?

Here, fought here,
once in ancient days and again
at the end of time?

<13>

5

First a visionary farmboy
dreaming in the fields still full of stumps,
along the dirt roads and among unpainted shacks,
the squat hay mows and churches
full of burnt-over believers.

Then a treasure-digger —
a conjure man with his witch hazel
divining rod, secret amulets
and a nose for gold.
He would demand a black sheep,
take it to the chosen spot
and lead the beast around in a circle
with its throat cut, trailing blood
to appease the evil spirits
guarding the treasure.

Next he appeared
as the high hillbilly wizard
with secret spectacles:
the Urim and Thummim,
two clots of glass fallen from the sky,
and a Magic Peepstone.
Like the Egyptians
who stared into the shine on a pool of ink,
Joseph stared into the sheen
on his seer stone,
glimpsing wondrous sights,
specters, infernal spirits,
mountains of gold and silver.

<14>

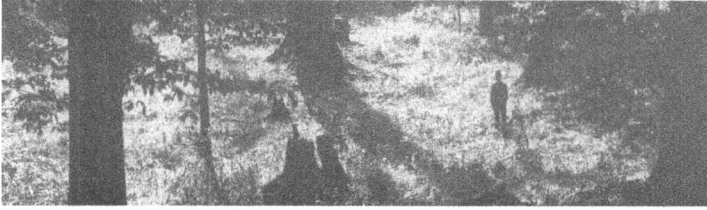

To his Latter Day Saints
he was the prophet of restoration,
"author and proprietor"
of the *Book of Mormon*
which made him a heretic, a renegado;
for a prophet is never honored
in his own country and among his kin
and in his own house.

And so he fled to the west
in January, in a sleigh.
Joseph with two acolytes
and Emma, his pregnant first wife.
Jingle bells muffled for stealth,
a furtive fleeing —
leaving behind, untended
the grave of Albion Brother.

And finally a desert warlord
with four dozen
flesh-wives and ghost-wives.
And he declared
to his followers:
"We will trample down our enemies
and make it one gore of blood
from the Rocky Mountains
to the Atlantic ocean.
I will be to this generation
a second Mohammed whose motto
in treating for peace was
'the Alcoran or the sword.'

<15>

So shall it eventually be
with us —
Joseph Smith or the Sword."

Until the end of his life —
shot to pieces
    by a vigilance mob —
he was followed, spectered,
haunted by the voice and face
and power
of Albion
his brother.

<16>

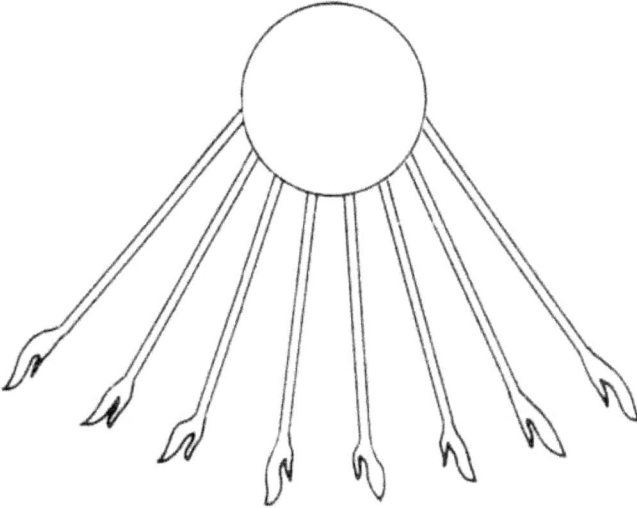

It's all plural.
Gods, the Elohim,
progressive beings
making their way up the ladder
to absolute divinity.
Solar systems, one for each saint
who has progressed to godhood.
Wives, forty-eight for the prophet,
a dozen or so each for the men
lower in the hierarchy.
Heavens, three degrees of glory, trinity of afterlives
— celestial, terrestrial and telestial —
containing souls greater in number
than all the grains of sand
in all the deserts of the world,
or all the crystals of salt

<17>

in all the unbreached horde-holes
beneath the world.

It's all plural.
The Shards of Ra:
the great solar god broken
into a billion billion pieces,
a stone disc shattered,
sunwheel spinning out of control:
shooting sparks, glowing fragments,
a billion billion stars,
meteors of war, molten gold gobbets,
the red hot tears of all the plural wives
full with child,

bright flecks of sweat
and human seed
jots of germ plasm
making life
making souls
making the endless
kingdoms come.

<18>

7

In this second year of 22,
after a century of occultation,
the earth moves again
and gives up its dead.
The earth shakes
and the mansions of the dead are opened.
After one hundred years of darkness,
silence, waiting,
the white light pours forth again.

The Prophet Smith proclaimed his truth:
The Great Restoration.
In 1822, he unearthed his golden plates
blinding with brightness, inscribed
in Reformed Egyptian script.
One hundred years later
the second dispensation begins.

In Alexandria, Ahmed Fuad assumes
the title, "King of Egypt."
For the first time in two and a half millennia
there is a king who can rightfully claim
the cobra crown.
Fuad is the first Egyptian
to rule the Mother of Nations since the day
the last Pharaoh was overthrown
by a Persian Warlord.
Then came Alexander the Great,
followed by more Greeks, the Ptolemaic kings.
Next came Roman conquerors, then Arabs,
then the Mamelukes, the Turks,
briefly the French and finally the British.

<19>

For 2,500 years Egypt had been the slave
    of foreign powers.
But in this year of 22
behold, a new dispensation is begun.
In Egypt, unto us
a king.

<20>

8

In Rome, in this same year,
Mussolini — *Il Duce* —
makes his march to power
in wing collar, cutaway coat and spats.
Behind him, thousand of *arditi* in black shirts,
jack boots, shoulders thrown back with pride,
heads held high, stride in columns
into the old Imperial City.

Within hours, the degenerate king
has accepted Mussolini as the new ruler.
Within hours, the Pope is cringing
on his knees, praying for *Il Duce*.
Within hours, news goes round the world

<21>

on buzzing wires:
a new power has risen to take its rightful place
among the nations of the world.

After two millennia, the fascist salute is reborn,
reclaimed from a statue
of a victorious Roman general,
right arm outstretched, rigid as a battering ram.
And the fasces itself —
a bundle of rods surrounding an ax,
bound together by leathern thongs —
the fasces is unveiled again,
marched through the Eternal City
carried by the new lictor,
giving its name to this ancient-future
tribal-imperial rebirth:
Fascismo.

<22>

The Man from Beyond is Houdini:
    World Famous Self-Liberator.
    The Greatest Mystifier that History Chronicles.
    The Supreme Ruler of Magic.
    The Master-Man of Mystery.
    The King of Escapologists.
And he appears on screen
as a man frozen for one hundred years
and chopped from a block of ice in 1922.

The Man From Beyond appears,
glowing with silver nitrite life,
breathing 20th century cinematic air
just as King Tut sees the sun —
Royal Ra — again
and feels his power, again.
Just as *Il Duce* declares
himself ruler of reborn Italy.
Just as Fuad takes the cobra throne
and stares out at his kingdom's
sand, sun-fire and emptiness.
The men from beyond:
    trapped in ice
    buried in ancient sand
    locked away in prison.
The lost kings of 22,
redeemed from death, return.

<23>

For the final spectacular scene
Houdini's movie crew goes to western York State,
to Niagara itself,
where he battles the rapids
to save one more
panting canoe maiden
— at the verge of the cataract —
from the plummet-death thunder,
crawling, soaked and beautiful, to safety
as thousands cheer
in shimmering darkness.

<24>

10

An apparition of Danites —
hunters of Latter Day heretics,
avenging angels, missionary assassins —
drifting into York State from the far west
to cleanse the sacred sites
to expunge all taint
from the holy lands, here in the nowhere
of humble Wayne County.
Silent men with Stetson hats
lizard skin boots
sunburnt faces
driving the back roads
through the Montezuma Swamp:
    Pilgrimport to Clyde to Savannah
through the Bristol Hills:
    Naples to Gulick to Italy
in powerful motorcars with license plates
always obscured by red-brown spatters
of dried distant mud.

<25>

One such automobile stops
at the four corners of Livonia Center.
A man with short gray whiskers
enters the general store, buys ten cents
of crackers and a can of sardines
and asks how far it is to Honeoye,
saying the name wrong,
marking himself as an outlander.

He produces a hand drawn map
and listens politely to the directions
while a boy peeks into the motorcar
and sees the back seat filled with
strange luggage:
suitcases made with bulges, tapers and bends
as though to transport ancient musical instruments,
or modern surgical equipment,
a machine gun or a magician's tools,
the ritual impedimenta of vengeance,
or perhaps the abortive products
of sacred taxidermy.

There are those who claim
the Danite Bands are a mere fabrication,
a slander on peace-loving saints
or the figment of diseased minds
which can not abide the truth.
And there are those who swear
that the Danites are as real
as a stiletto in the dark
or a single gunshot heard a half mile away
across the dry rattling of late autumn corn.

<26>

What is known for certain is this —
a blood oath was sworn by Latter Day Saints
a blood oath on backsliders and apostates,
sayers of lies and makers of false statements,
a blood oath against those who turn their backs
on the prophet's gods and the precepts of his church,
on those who say secrets
where the ears of infidels might be listening.

What has been seen is less certain —
plumes of dust above a far-off roadway,
the foundation and chimney spine
of a shack burnt last week to the ground,
a dog strangled with its own chain,
smoke, shadow,
a glint of copper in the weeds.

<27>

11

There are places where no roads reach
no electric lights burn
no officers of the law
come to force children into schools.
In the Montezuma Swamp
rattlesnakes still nest and breed
and hunt and kill.
In the Bristol Hills
people still say the word "shilling"
when they mean a twenty-five cent piece
and "welkin" when they speak of the sky.
In these places
there remain masters of the divining rod
for sinking a well
and masters of the rifle
for getting short meat
to the table.

The capital at Albany,
though only 200 miles away,
could just as easily be
Peking or Paris,
Berlin or Bangalore,
for all the influence
it has on these places.
Manhattan might as well be Oz
or an airless empty metropolis
on the far, cold, dark side of the moon.
Telephone, radio, moving picture
and phonograph machines are as alien
to the people here
as the spaceships and rayguns
of a Barsoomian tale.

<28>

But deadly reptiles and the northern lights,
Spencer rifles, water-witching
and The Redemption of the Dead —
these remain.
These are real.

<29>

12

Albion emerges —
stiff and crystal-crusted
from the white grave.
Every year for a century,
Albion has grown in size and power.
Now deep in the salt mines,
Italian shovel men and hammer men
claw their way toward him
in the largest salt mine on the planet,
right there lying in the bed
of the Genesee valley.

The Italians in Retsof
and Piffardinia swing hammers
in the glittering chambers,
breathing briny tomb dust,
singing tunes from *Aïda*
grand Italian Egypto,
dreaming of distant Fascismo,
of King Fuad and King Tut too
who, in this year of 22,
is exhumed, roused
from his millennial sleep.

In the new world,
Tutankhamen's brother-corpse
— his brother-monarch —
rises with no gold, and no jewels
no crown, only earthly armor:
salt crust harder than steel,
whiter than ice, snow, chalk,
teeth or bone.

<30>

Albion the giant rises
and calls his followers
to rise likewise:
from seething swamps
from groaning mineshafts
from smoke-blurred valleys
from green graves long untended.

<31>

13

A revival:
a bringing back of the dead
a raising forth of the old
the hidden, the lost
the one and the only.

Loud pleading plangent voices —
yammering prayers to Thor and Thoth
Isis and Osiris and the All-Night
Left-Handed Jesus of the Genesee.
Gyrations and gibberings and hot sweaty palms.
In the pages of the *Wayne Sentinel*
are reports of "racial degenerates"
and worshippers of an "Iroquois Reptile God,"
of strange comings and goings,
disturbances of the peace and of white-cowled men
walking the back roads of the Bristol Hills
and the trails that wind
through the Montezuma Swamp.

In safe little village churches,
Methodists and Baptists
Presbyterians and Lutherans
snore through sermons
and groan through hymns
that once rang loud as a fire bell.
The weakest Jesus in the universe
floats in these tepid waters,
little more than a glowing wisp
with his pale halo, wan smile,
perfectly clean gown
and pretty blond hair.

<32>

Only ten miles away,
down at the end of a dirt track,
another Jesus is raised from the dead.
On Pentecost, called Whitsuntide,
in these days of 22,
the old chant rises:

> *Salt, sugar, snow and cream*
> *chalk and milk, a cloud of steam*
> *onion, potato, a fat moonstone*
> *eggs and ice, teeth and bone.*

Raising the vasty god:
the giant Salt-Jesus of Albion —
a subterranean form whose grave
once stretched from the cliffs of Dover
to the Hebrides,
from the fens of Lincolnshire
to the Irish Sea.
But who now rises
from his bed of crystals
in the new world.

He comes forth
swinging the sledge hammer,
instrument of his doom —
reclaimed, redeemed.
This Savior is missing a couple of fingers.
He's scarred, sweat-stained, crusty
and burnt by the sun.

<33>

And he's not afraid to wade into the swamp muck,
stick his hands in, grab a rattler
and bang its head against a rock
to show him who's boss.

This is Jesus-Albion-Thor
the white man's groundshaking specter
anger-god, hammer-god, hunger-god
big as a thunderhead,
crimson-faced as sunset over the
Genesee Valley in August,
louder than angelic drumfire.

<34>

14

Question:
Would Iroquois worship snakes?
Would they wear the white cowl
and domino robe,
set up the fiery Tau cross
on lost York State valley crests?
Would Senecas and Cayugas talk about being
a "white and delightsome" race?
Would they confuse the terms "Pharaoh" and "Fascism"
or worship the floodwaters of the Genesee
as fellahin worship the black fertile ooze
of the Nile?

Answer:
No, these are not a degenerate people,
not mongrel Indians,
but the original true believers
forced by gentile preachers
and the specter of Danite vengeance
to hide their truth,
driven away from Cumorah
— the Holy Hill —
from the Sacred Grove and the Smith Farm,
into the wilds of the Montezuma swamp
and the misty valleys of the Bristol Hills.

<35>

Conclusion:
Like the original followers of Jesus
and Mohammed, the first believers
had hearts full of heavenly fire.
It wasn't Albion Smith
who created the most vapid church in the universe,
but the later Latter Day Saints
who captured heavenly fire in paltry vessels
of human making, who trapped holy thunderbolts
and made them
weak as buzzing lightning bugs
in a fruit jar.

<36>

15

Whitsuntide, 1922
White Sunday:
a second, American, Pentecost
when the new Holy Ghost comes
in tongues of salt and fire,
and a thousand jabbering voices
are united into one solid
sacred sameness
and true believers put on
the robes of purity.

The Invisible Empire
marches down Main Street,
gathers to rout out, finally,
the remnant of the heretic seed.
White knights burn crosses on hilltops
to call the clans to battle.
Fire on high, fire below.
War now, war then, war always.
White American Legions march —
hailing King Fuad, in the Egypt of now
hailing King Tut, in the Egypt of then
hailing *Il Duce*, who shall conquer
the Egypt of always —
Fascismo staking its claim
on the pharaoh's heart.

<37>

Singing:
O Isis and Osiris, send us
in the brilliancy of the meridian sun
triumphal music for American Fascismo.
White cowls, black shirts
and crimson choir robes.
In Salt Lake City they sing
"The Battle Hymn of the Republic"
four hundred strong —
a white and delightsome chorus.
This, however, will not drown out
the louder, cruder, stronger, raw hymns
that once rang from the tops of drumlins
and ridge crests. It cannot drown
the birth-groans of Albion Salt
from the far side of the continent.

<38>

16

Thus speaks the prophet:
blindness can be too much illumination
or not enough,
a superabundance of light
as well as its total absence.
Stare into the face
of thrice-great Ra
— the visible-invisible god —
stare long and hard
and you will go God-blind.

I, the prophet, proclaim:
the existence of three heavens
and three holy kings of the sun.
Black Ra —
Lord of the terrestrial heaven.
Red Ra —
who rules the telestial regions.
White Ra —
celestial monarch, noon's great potentate.

Black Ra —
the king of night
the sun as it moves through darkness,
through the underwater, underground realms,
the solar serpent making its way
through slime, slough, caverns,
the vast swamp of night.

<39>

Red Ra —
born in the horizon's feverish throb
and dying in the same crimson sky-wound,
the sun-scarab who makes his flaming
exit and entrance
from he womb of night
and back again.

White Ra —
the sunwheel turning across the sky
burning a hole in the blue,
in human eyes,
a perfect roundness
a permanent meridian absence,
hot, high and forever empty.

Thus speaks the prophet:
Blindness is neither curse nor blessing,
slavery nor freedom
but the imprint of Holy Ra's face —
dark, burning and devoid,
black, red and white.
Go then, God-blind
into the world.
And conquer.

<40>

17

Once on Cumorah Hill
the lost races
— Lamanites and Nephites —
met to destroy each other,
to fight the last great battle.

Once, where this quiet farmland now rolls,
thousands and thousands and ten times
thousands of warriors,
dark-skinned, copper-skinned and light,
stormed up and over
this sacred drumlin.
Race war in ancient America —
race war, seen in a vision by the prophet
and written down
by the hand of Mormon.

> *And it came to pass that they did fall upon my people*
> *with the sword and with the bow*
> *and with the arrow and with the axe*
> *and with all manner of weapons of war.*

> *And their flesh and bones and blood*
> *lay upon the face of the earth*
> *being left by the hands of those who slew them*
> *to molder upon the land and to crumble*
> *and to return to their mother earth.*

> *And it came to pass that after the great*
> *and tremendous battle at Cumorah, behold:*
> *the Nephites who had escaped into the country*
> *southward were hunted by the Lamanites*
> *until they were destroyed.*

<41>

And my father also was killed by them
and I even remain alone to write
the sad tale of the destruction of my people.
But behold: they are gone
and I fulfill the commandment of my father.
And whether they will slay me
I know not.

<42>

18

Salt to salt. East to west.
The thickest, the richest, the truest
— the best vein of salt in the whole world —
lies dead center beneath the birthplace
of the Latter Day empire.
And the vastness of the Great Salt Lake
stands as the end point
of the final, primal Mormonic trek.
Salt to salt. West to east.
The soldier of god and the warrior priest.

A golden angel stands at the peak
of Cumorah, Moroni with his trumpet
calling the armies of the lost east
out of their graves.
Another shimmering angel,
another Moroni, stands at the peak
of the temple in Salt Lake City,
calling the armies of the found west
to battle formation
to march back along the Great Salt Axis,
back to the holy hill
where the heretics, the scum
and offscourings of Albion
— the first and the last —
have gathered.

<43>

19

Once more on Cumorah hill
the least, the last, the lost
stand in ragged battle formation.
They stand to meet the Danite horde
and the American knights of the white cross,
the warriors of the Invisible Empire
— invisible no more —
self revealed, self-proclaimed avengers
fighting the final battle
again.

Out of the west come dust devils,
ghost riders in the sky,
a swarm of biplanes with hieroglyphic amulets
gleaming on their wings.
Coming in low, over the hill
with machine guns nattering
and hand-tossed dynamite bombs
shaking the obelisk
where golden Moroni yet stands
blowing the herald trumpet,
though unheard in the ground-thunder
and sky-quakes of the bombardment.
Moroni calls forward his Danite legions,
phalanxes of brawny half-naked musselmen
and stripling youth, calling out
"Joseph Smith or the sword!"

Then, looming vast as Kolob
comes the Grand Dragon's command ship —
golden zeppelin of the sun.

<44>

In the gondola, the Latter Day prophet
wearing Napoleonic braids and epaulets,
with his sword banging at his thigh,
sights through binoculars and gives the order:
"All American legions forward.
Joseph Smith or the sword!"

Western cowboys with sunburnt skin
push back the pallid natives of the gloomy east,
gunslingers savaging the savages,
bathing in the blood of crypto-apostates.
White-robed legions make the stiff-armed salute,
their hearts lifted by song.
Mine eyes have seen the glory.
But now they see the specter too —
Old Glory's green slime shadow,
a caustic cloud rolling down the hill.
They scream and tear
as vile ichor oozes over them.
Chlorine and mustard gas
making the sky into an ocean
and the ground into a sea bed.
The zeppelin looms nearer
like a great battleship
seen from beneath,
blotting out the hill with its ovoid shadow,
floating in a fungous death-cloud,
the dirigible of the gods.

<45>

20

Only tongues and a plowshare
only exhausted lungs, silenced prayers, forbidden spells
written and burnt in the forests of the night,
only the ghost of temple bells
the sour reek of snuffed candles
the specter of human sacrifice
divine occultation.

Only a fragment twist of copper
turned over in the fresh-broken field.
Crows circle, shouting, seeing the glint
where plowshare caught the relic,
scraping a new bright edge
that catches the sun.

Albion sleeps again,
defeated and yet still the victor.
Frost burnt off by the sun
turns to vapor, the breath of dawn
rising into the icy blue sky.
His brother too is vanquished, into his own smoke
and brilliant ego-gleam.
"As man now is
God once was."
Prophet, president, solar potentate -
the lord now of his own galaxy.

No more chains to drag up the forefathers.
No more coaxing the nubile wife-hordes.
They come willingly, joyously, freely -
streaming in luminous angel rivers
across the void.
No more revelations.
No more secret treaties with the dead.

<46>

There is just the white serpent now,
coiled on itself in a square-walled lair
of wet clods and coffin clay,
a lunar white creature in Albion's dighole
damp with ground ooze,
tangled root hairs and root fingers.
Albion, first and last prophet,
extends his glistening tongue
to taste broken earth, the vapor of lies,
the fear and need of his long-gone brother.
He sucks in a whiff of the new sky
and expels one reptilian breath —
his hydrogen hiss.

There at the Smith family's heavenly hole —
not a stairway to the sun
or ladder to the stars
but a path downward, inward.
There at the lip of the grave
which the plow broke open and forgot.
There in cornfield sunlight,
the fragile scroll of history
glows briefly and crumbles to ash.
A cold wind burns the truth to dust.
White flakes scatter in the furrows
which even the crows ignore.

Far off, the tractor engine
mutters and curses
stutters and seizes
    — backfires —
one dull rifle-shot
killing the horse power,
and itself
goes dead.

The prophet in his Golden Bible
told of a fiery white Jesus
appearing in the New World —
proclaiming a new dispensation.
This was his only true prophesy,
though a vision of the future, not the past.
It was no giant phosphorescent Jesus
who crossed the Atlantic
after his resurrection,
who appeared in the sky
as the holy magnesium flare.

It was and it is and it shall be
Albion the salt specter,
seen one hundred years in the future,
who reaches up, grabs the zeppelin
in both hands, and crushes it.
Iron ribs snap, canvas skin tears,
a wailing cloud of hydrogen billows out.
And with one touch of Albion's glittering tongue,
the airship explodes into a second sun,
King Ra's fiery heart
enveloping the earth, the sky, past and future.
Albion and his brother
united in flame
now and forever
amen.

<48>

PART II: ROMMEL AND CALIGARI

1

A sunwheel cross hangs in the palm branches —
four stiff spokes, four bent black arms
reaching for nothing.
Stolen from a distant Aryan dreamland,
smuggled to Europe, and held captive forever.
The broken cross turns in the sky,
a right angle vortex expelling energies.
Copper coils spin in the magnetic fields
to generate heat, light, motion
and Germanic germ plasm.
Broken cross suspended from the tree of life.

Hermes Trismegistus — Thrice Great Hermes —
called the sun The Visible God.
Hermes the magician,
multiplier of time and ruler of fates,
divine scribe, who gave the written word,
who measured the world,
dividing all Egypt,
which is the world and the word,
into sacred units
of distance and destiny.
Hermes the name-giver
named the sun
and its two-dimensional surrogate
The Visible God.

<51>

2

In Rome, they worship human gods again —
Caesar, Scipio, *Il Duce*.
They carry the fasces
and make the stiff-armed imperial salute,
fingers rigid, shouting like war-dogs.
Il Duce bellows back at his black shirt legions
and the lictor marches past
carrying the new fasces,
emblem of newborn Roman power,
the throb of ego and cinematic war-lust.
He relives the triumphs of Scipio Africanus,
his vision of himself
reborn as the invincible Roman general.
The most expensive Italian film ever made
a vast and bloated kino behemoth
fascist Rome's salute to itself
grandfather of every sword and sandal epic
featuring Hercules, Samson and Maciste.

You must see: *Scipio Africanus — The Defeat of Hannibal*.
Fifty elephants slaughtered on the screen and
a cast of ten thousand mock warriors
practicing for their real deaths in the real African desert
under the true African sun.

<52>

3

Like Caesar
Il Duce wanted the Pharaoh's heart
and his heartland:
Suez — pyramids — Alexandrian magic — white gold
the delta with its countless acres of cotton,
black peasants stoop-backed in the Nile-rich fields.
Mussolini's pincers — Ethiopia and Libya —
    poised to crush Egypt.
A half million Italian soldiers
led by General Bombastico —
with his ludicrous mustachios,
tarnished braid and rattling epaulets,
an opera buffo buffoon —
marched fifty miles toward Cairo
then stopped to dig in.

Outnumbered ten to one
the British counterattacked from Egypt
sweeping up a hundred thousand prisoners,
four hundred battle tanks,
a thousand heavy guns.
And other, finer, Italian spoils of war:
bed sheets, silk shirts, Florentine leather toilet seats,
spiced hair pomades, wines and liqueurs
and a caravan of Neapolitan harlots
jabbering and shameless as jays.

Within days, nothing was left of *Il Duce*'s army
but columns of trucks speeding west,
thousands of men throwing down their rifles,
running in blind panic through the dunes.

<53>

4

Far to the north
the half-blind God of Rage
breaks his chains,
climbs down from the World-Tree
and summoning Rommel to HQ
gives the command:
Go to Afrika — with the K, the K, the K.
Afrika with a K is the Caligari Continent.
The father of madness, the almighty hypnotist,
pronounces doom on the puny British outpost,
waves his gnarled fist and sends two divisions
— 15th Panzer and 5th Light —
to the sun-crusted desert
no less an alien landscape than Mars
or Hell.

No Valhalla in the Sahara.
No beautiful armored battle maidens
for these doomed warriors.
No Thor or Freya,
Balder or Loki.
No All-Father Wotan
with his pack of blood-mad sons.
The Gods of the snow
evaporate here
like frost in burning dawn
or nightdew on the blacksmith's forge.
In the north Afrikan dust
there are other, older, obscurer
gods, who must be placated, obeyed,
and offered human sacrifice.
They loom oblique and distant —
incandescent at dusk
and spectral at noon.

<54>

5

The All-Father
hung on the tree for three days,
gave up an eye for wisdom
gave up half of all light and vision,
died and was reborn hanging.

<56>

Now, another god descends —
one half Wotan and one half Caligari.
Nordic war-father and carnival charlatan.
Eternal on the screen, descending
from the clouds, from heaven to earth
in *The Triumph of the Will.*
Torchlight parades at Nuremberg, massed bands,
a sea of chanting true believers
a pulsing ocean of
stiff-armed salutes.

These are the boys who marched once in the forest.
These were the Wandervogel,
with guitars and wooden flutes,
folks songs, camaraderie, tramping the trails.
Nature boys, heavenly youth.
These were the ones who worshipped
the northern sun,
burnt brown boys now desert-blackened men.
Soldiers under the sign of palm tree
and sunwheel cross.

<57>

6

And Rommel to lead them.
Erwin Johannes Eugen Rommel.
Peaked cap, clean shaven jaw,
trench coat, goggles against the dust.
On his chest the eagle whose talons hold
the swastika,
which means nothing
to him.
Four broken radial lines.
Rommel is the human vector of force —
isolated, utterly alone.
This is his essence:
not ideology, race or politics.
This is war in the 4th dimension
where distances and barriers,
magnitude and direction, are redefined
moment by moment.
Minions of the enemy god mass against him.
The enemy — not human life
but objects to be destroyed —
objectives to be achieved.
These pure diagonals, this straightedge roadway,
this N-degree elevation, these absolute planes
    of sheer rock.
Escape into the abstraction of G:
Geometry, Germania, Guderian,
Gravitation and Gods.

<58>

7

Cranes lift the tanks off transport ships in Libya —
Panzer Armee Afrika arriving from the fourth dimension.
All the angles are wrong.
Teutonic cubist war machines descend —
skewed, canted to a higher level geometry.
Turrets, caterpillar treads, snub-nosed cannon,
water and gas tanks strapped on the sides.
They rev and roar as they're hoisted
down to touch the seething sand.
Bang-steel beetles
crusted with chevrons, crosses,
insignia with the sharp-edged look of the Caligari film set.
The alphanumeric markings
— Kfz 222, PZKW Mark IV —
are secret formulae,
spells against the blinding Khamsin,
against British bombers
and bad luck.

<59>

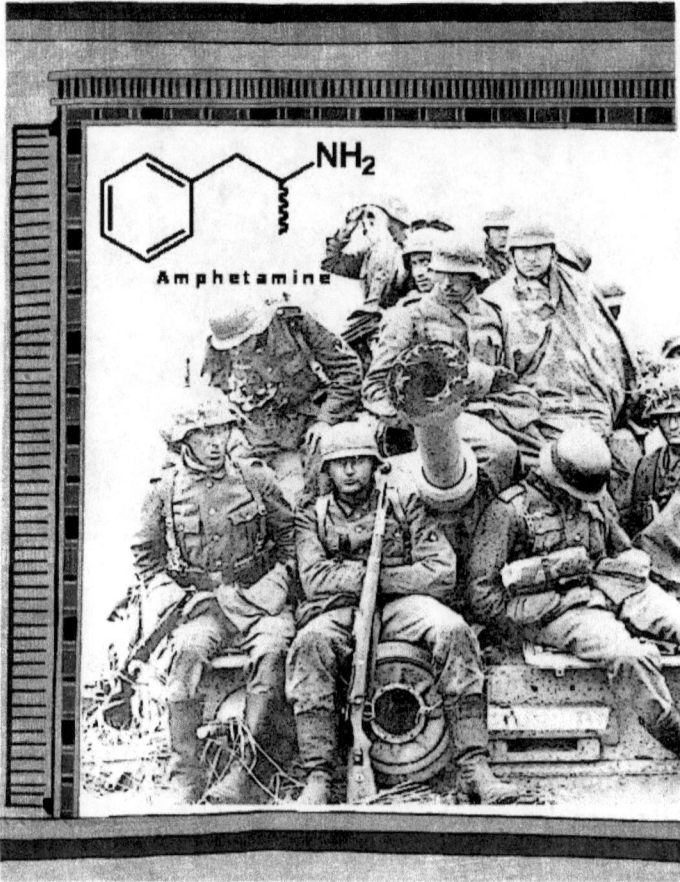

<60>

8

Immediately —
without waiting for reinforcements
or orders from on high —
he attacks.
Phantom Armee Afrika:
half the tanks are VW dummies
to fool the British reconns,
wooden bodies on Volkswagen scarab cars.
The other half are real —
armed and armored, but no less an illusion.

Combat as a sand-colored blur.
Lightning strikes, bomber runs, Rommel's half-track:
centaur vehicle part truck and part battle tank
with the general peering out the top.

Binoculars for farseeing, radio trucks,
Rommel's own light airplane
for swooping down on his own troops.
And always the groan and grind of killing machines
in the seething mirage heat.

Within two weeks he had retaken Libya
and crossed the Egypt line.

<61>

9

Ancient dust roils around the tank treads
which criss and cross, making alligator skin of the desert.
Here Roman legions marched,
Alexander's army too,
Hannibal's foot soldiers and Mohammed's cavalry.
An endless ebb and flow of sun-blackened men.
Their footprints, wheel tracks,
sand-scoured armor
and blasted engines,
their bones.
All of these have disappeared.

Light-skinned men from the far north
all of them burnt to the core.
Germans and English roasted by the sun.
Blonds and redheads
from Saxony and New Zealand,
Canada, the Transvaal, the Rhineland,
the hills of Wales and the mountains of Bavaria.
Cooks, truck drivers, radio operators and navigators,
sappers, gunners and reconns.
The lowly mechanic —
hands coated with gear grease.
No water to wash with and no point in washing.

Scottish bagpipers go into battle
their blistered scream barely heard above the diesel roar.
Sun-maddened Axis men hallucinate
    Euro-Egyptian operas.

<62>

The Italians sing from *Aïda*
and the Germans from *The Magic Flute.*
Du musst Sarastro werden.
You must become Mozart's Pharaonic wizard.
The stage sky: the inner vault of a refiner's furnace.
Thirst so severe that men dream
of drinking their own blood
and gasoline.

<63>

10

To: ALL COMMANDERS AND CHIEFS OF STAFF
From: HEADQUARTERS, B.T.E. and M.E.F.

There exists a real danger that our friend Rommel
is becoming a kind of magician or bogeyman
    to our troops,
who are talking far too much about him.
He is by no means a superman,
although he is undoubtedly very energetic and able.
Even if he were a superman, it would still be
    highly undesirable
that our men should credit him with supernatural powers.

I wish to dispel by all possible means
the idea that Rommel represents something more
than an ordinary German general.
The important thing now is to see that we not
always talk of Rommel when we mean
    the enemy in Libya.
We must refer to "the Germans" or "the Axis powers"
or "the enemy" and not always keep harping on Rommel.

Please ensure that this order is put
into immediate effect.
And impress upon all commanders that,
from a psychological point of view,
it is a matter of the highest importance.

General C.J. Auchinleck
Commander-in-chief
Mediterranean Expeditionary Force

<64>

11

In 1920, Dr. Caligari emerged
from his clinging cocoon,
pulled back the trembling shadows,
brushed aside the film of darkness.
Caligari, master of magnetic sleep,
released his private somnambulist,
the homicidal clairvoyant Conrad Veidt.

<65>

White face with black smears around his eyes,
black lipstick, maniac leer, black tights
like a nightmare acrobat.
A zombie in a box —
a sex-killer in his own private coffin:
the Cabinet of Dr. Caligari.

Twenty years later he reappeared
on the North Afrikan Coast
in *Casablanca*, as Major Strasser
pronouncing his sneered doom on the allies:
"Round up the usual suspects."
And in *The Thief of Baghdad* too,
as the vicious grand vizier Jaffar.
But in 1920 he was the automaton Cesare,
the murder-minion of Caligari.

Adolf Butenandt, Berlin biochemist,
saw Dr. Caligari repeatedly that year.
And saw the words of doom
imprinted on the world.
In the penultimate scene,
where madness becomes manifest,
one commandment, one overpowering spell,
appears on city walls,
in the sky, in the gutter:

Du musst Caligari werden.
You must become Caligari.

<66>

Butenandt spent the rest of the decade
isolating male sex hormones.
Success came in 1931
after boiling 25,000 liters of fresh hot urine
collected from Berliner policemen
and distilling out their manly essence.

In 1939, as the German panzerfaust
tore out the heart of Poland,
came Butenandt's final triumph:
creating synthetic testosterone.
No distillate of hulking lawman piss
but pure, crystalline and absolute —
another German white powder of power.
For which the biochemist was awarded a Nobel,
though forces were at work to keep him from
claiming the Swedish prize until
hostilities had ended
and the nation of somnambulists
was back neatly, back safely,
in its box.

<67>

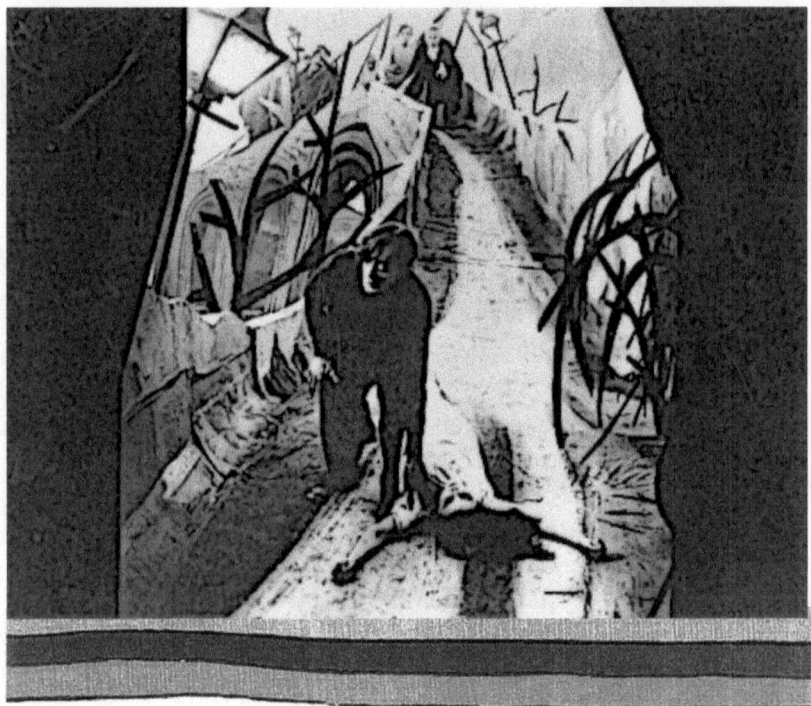

12

No right angles in the Caligari Universe,
no truly flat surfaces, no straight up or straight down.
Non-Euclidean vision creates
parallel lines which meet,
curved space and cyclical time.
In the world of Caligari, shadows are not
cast by physical objects
but painted permanently on the walls.
Converging vectors show us who is mad
and who stands outside of madness.

<68>

No points, but tiny inky holes.
No lines, but scars in the skin of the world.
Corkscrew dimensions, hyperbolic flatness
and twisted gravity.

Fissured, fractured vision:
wild faces irising in and out,
black flowers which blossom and die
in a moment.
Inter-titles between the shots
twitching like an amphetamine eyelid.
Far too many exclamation points.
Far too long on the screen.
Barbed messages —
letters as thorns and words as weapons
and pronouncements as entire invasions.
We read them and read them
and read them again.

Finally the word is gone
and the world returns to the screen:
a dwarf with bandy legs,
two policemen in squashed fezzes,
a dangling black skeleton,
a human shadow creeping along the wall,
the scientist as carnival barker
and sleepwalking lovers
lost in a permanent dream
of curved space and cyclical time.

<69>

13

Hermes Trismegistus called Egypt
the Widow of the Gods.
They died and she lived on,
mourning, always mourning.
Little Napoleon could not resist
bringing his little army there
to fight in the great shadow of the pyramids.
His gunners did not shoot the nose off the Sphinx.
That desecration belongs to a Moslem
who thought the Sphinx a vile heathen idol.
Tomb robbers, mummy-hunters, wakers of the dead
trickled into Egypt after Napoleon had fled.
The French built the Suez canal
and the Khedive Ismail paid for his own *Aïda*,
three nights of high Egypto flummery
to celebrate the great opening.

Sixty years later
Rommel, alone, stands on another stage
on an empty road in Libya
gazing toward that beautiful mirage:
the Pharaoh's phantom heart.
Hands behind his back
face shadowed by the brim of his cap,
grim set of the jaw,
boots to the knees and riding breeches.
Not a battered tank or truck in sight.
Just Rommel, standing absolutely alone,
ready to battle all the way there by himself.

<70>

No rest — just the fight —
no reward — just the lonely war.
On the road to Alexandria and Suez and perhaps India.
Between this nowhere and that endpoint
lies el Alamein
where he knows he will be defeated.
No end to the campaign, no linear history
but an endless replaying,
the same battle of iron shadows.

<71>

14

The 8th Army waits behind its wire.
Northumbrians, Yorkshiremen, Scots,
Indians, Australians
behind the magic line, waiting for Rommel.
Barbed wire divides the desert —
strings doubled, tripled, quadrupled —
millions of tiny stabbing seeds
rattling loose in the Khamsin.
And below the line, landmines
planted like bulbs in the lifeless dust
to blossom in brilliant fluorescence
of flame and shrapnel.
An instant,
then an empty
steel husk
twice dead.

After the battle,
broken shreds of wire gather themselves
into knots, then ghostly balls, then hyperspheres,
tumbleweeds rolling across the vastness,
the flatness, the emptiness of pure space.

<72>

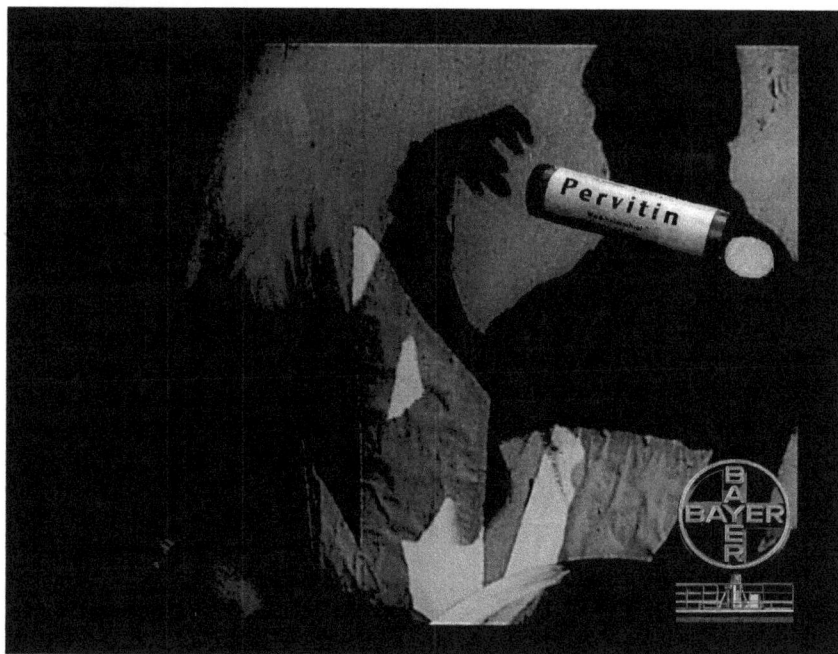

15

Three forms of esoteric power
made the Blitzkrieg possible:
    the theory of rapid, deep penetration
      war machines twice as fast and deadly as their enemies
      and chemical alteration of military consciousness.
The conquest of Poland, Denmark, Norway,
Belgium, Holland and France
was based as much on amphetamines as on radical
theories of war or occult machines of destruction.

In 1938, on the eve of the Blitzkrieg,
Temmler Pharmaceutical introduced its brand
of methamphetamine, called Pervitin.

<73>

In April, May and June of 1940
— as the Wehrmacht shot through France
and nearly eradicated the entire British Army —
German troops consumed
35,000,000 hits of Pervitin: little pills
sometimes called White Crosses
full of energy, stamina, clarity
and fighting spirit.
Paratroopers, British newspapers reported,
were landing behind enemy lines
"heavily drugged, fearless and berserk."

In the Spring of 1941 Allied intelligence
reported that the Germans were shipping 50 tons
of frozen adrenal glands from South America
in a gigantic submarine, to manufacture hormones
that would allow Luftwaffe airmen to perform
superhuman feats of flying and killing.
The prospect of *Übermensch* pilots exalted
on artificial testosterone, adrenal extracts,
hypervitamins and "Stuka Tablets"
sent a shockwave of fear through the British
High Command.

In August of 1942,
when General Montgomery arrived in Egypt,
he was already a convert to the Way of Speed.
Convinced that the 8th Army lacked fighting spirit
for the needed all-out assault against Rommel,
he added amphetamines to his arsenal.
For open-throttle tank charges,
for near-suicidal infantry attacks against
the most feared forces in the German army,
the British soldiers needed a jolt
of artificial manhood, bravery and aggression.

<74>

Convinced he must throw everything he had
    against Rommel,
Montgomery ordered Benzedrine supplied
to all the combat units under his command:
one hundred thousand tablets of speed
for the initial attack on the Afrika Korps
at el Alamein.

<75>

16

Rommel was known to go
fifty hours straight with no sleep.
Dr. Caligari never slept at all
or at least was never seen to do so.
Cesare, his somnambulist, never truly awoke,
even when his eyes fluttered open
and he emerged from his cabinet
and his cold hands clenched
around the neck of a beautiful girl.

The Northmen had no god of sleep.
And so, in Libya and Egypt, they prayed
to dark southern deities,
to Hypnos and Somnus and Anubis
whose silent howling echoed across the desert.
But most of all to Hermes-Thoth,
Lord of the Moon, medicine and the realm of the dead,
guide of souls through the Night Land.

When Rommel did shut his eyes,
his sleep dissolved the world,
drowning out artillery,
washing away the screams of dying men
and falling Stukas,
flooding the Sahara with oceanic oblivion.
When Caligari merged with the shadows,
visions crowded around him like god-sick spirits
clamoring for release,
or the ghost of Euclid, haunted by hyperspheres
which he declared to be impossible.

<76>

When Cesare rose from his coffin-bed,
he was still a slave to his master's
magic, his magnetic force.
And he still slept —
though his eyes were open
and he seemed to see.

<77>

17

In Alexandria by the sea, Hermes Trismegistus
compiled his book of sacred lore:
The Corpus Hermeticum.
There we find
prophecy, alchemical wisdom,
astronomy and astrology,
incantations and divinations,
sunwheels and heart symbols,
medicine for the soul as well as for the body,
magical utterances and perverse arcana,
cosmic geometry, invocations of the dream-god.
And amulets against:
plague, poison, ugliness,
the wrong kind of madness,
the lust for gold,
powerful enemies and weak-willed friends,
pride, hunger, pestilence and lies.

Rommel came within striking distance of Alexandria.
His Mark IIIs and Mark IVs, his 88 mm guns
could be heard, a distant nightmare muttering,
all the way to the Ras al-Tin palace.
Rommel knew nothing of Thrice-Great Hermes
yet he carried the god in his body.
He felt the god-weight of the secret book,
the aura of the secret words,
the spells for and the spells against.

<78>

18

In the false dawn's glimmering, he wakes
and feels the rumble of his armored columns.
He hears diesel engines
the clank and clatter of tank treads
gears grinding desert grit
air filters choked and panting.
He knows the truth
but does not curse the luck that's shifted against him,
the maps and plans and orders
which all prove useless and illusory now.
As one who knew all along,
who had the foresight and courage to see the end,
he says instead, "It is so."
There: the defeat that approaches.
He does not make himself small
with blame and recrimination.
As one who knew all along
as the man chosen to lead and to triumph and to fail,
he rises from his cot,
pulls back the stiff flap on the tent
and watches the spectral parade.
No false emotion.
No bravado, empty courage, rage.

Only grief —
which is true.
He watches the ragged columns moving out
toward dawn, and defeat.
He hears the shadow thunder,
the bleak grieving music of that last assault
and says goodbye to it all,
the life he is losing.

<79>

19

The battle began in thunder and ended in rain.
Between them lay three days of fire.
Two hundred thousand civilized men made savage —
burnt, buried, blasted into being
and then blown away like dust.
First, silence and a full moon
so bright it hurt the eyes.
Then on Montgomery's command
in an instant, bright and night reversed themselves,
his bombardment shattering all the windows in heaven,
shards of black mirror glass falling
falling.

Men made mad
by Benzedrine and Pervitin
by the endless pounding of the earth and sky drums
by the caustic stench of high explosives.
In an hour the gunners are all deaf
and their gloves burnt through
by the heat of cannon barrels.
900 British guns
firing 900 rounds per minute
into the German minefields at el Alamein.
Beating the earth
beating the flesh,
drums made
of human skulls
the size of the moon
and sticks from the thigh bones of giants.

<80>

Concussion, percussion, confusion, profusion.
The pouring out of fiery spirits.
Continuous muzzle flash carves black masks
onto white Northmen faces
then strips them off
revealing the red
weeping
nerve tissue beneath.

After the barrage comes the sweeping of the minefields:
five hundred sappers stumbling through
    the seared darkness
searching for shrapnel S-mines the size of a tin can
and fat black Teller mines
and jury-rigged aerial bombs now buried in the earth
waiting for the pressure of a tank tread or a footstep.
The sappers lay 88,000 lamps to set off the cleared zones
and 120 miles of marker tape.
When the sweeper booms conk out,
the sappers go on their hands and knees
stabbing the earth with bayonets to find the mines
and dig them out
with their hands.

Montgomery wanted more fighting spirit
and got Benzedrine specters —
the freezing burn in the brain.
His hundred thousand men thrust forward
and for three days the armies raged,
throbbed, merged and split, dissolved and congealed,
breathed the hot reek of diesel and desert sweat
pulverized rock, vaporized blood, adrenaline, exhaustion,
pulp marrow, burnt hair and dead god meat.

<81>

Half his army evaporated
and the other half still hallucinating.
After three days on amphetamines and fire,
the mind boils over like a radiator
spilling its luminous slime,
heat and cold reversed, hissing overload,
white tremors in the dark neural matter.
Pill-cooled, pill-cooked retinas
see dust devils as the enemy
see a severed hand crawling in the moonlight
see tanks driving sideways
see a refrigerator truck full of bottled blood
marked by the sign of gigantic vampire bat.

Even in victory, the British shake and gibber.
Even as the Germans retreat
in the bone cold of utter loss,
the Eighth Army stands motionless in the rain.
Beetle-hard souls crouch in their holes
crying out for just one moment of silence,
one second so that their nerves can breathe.
Then their fingers twitch on the triggers.
They fire on their own men, or at the sky itself:
knocking loose a spatter
of heaven's icy tears.

<82>

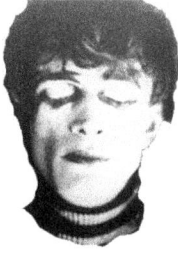

20

Conrad Veidt, Cesare, Major Strasser
and the Grand Vizier Jaffar
all died, at the same moment —
a foursome at the 8th hole
of the Riviera Country Club in Hollywood.
An actor who'd fled the old world to escape the swastika.
A murderous sleepwalker, trapped forever in dreamland.
A Nazi officer played by a vehement anti-Nazi.
A Persian schemer with turban, flowing robes
            and a California tan.
All of them the same man —
all of them dead
April 3, 1943.

Exactly as Rommel left Afrika
and the Afrika Korps.
Lies, slander and poisonous guesses
surround his return to the Fatherland.
Some hinted that he saw the inevitable defeat
and fled to save himself the shame of capture.
Some said that Mussolini demanded his departure.
Some wondered about the wounds, the bandages
    on his throat
and the desert sores on his face.

<83>

Rommel told his family this:
he returned to the Northland for permission
to withdraw all his troops, to save their lives
and abandon their machinery of war.

When this permission was denied
he asked to return to Afrika.
This request too was refused.

Two weeks later
the Afrika Korps fought its last battle,
outside of Tunis, without its leader
and surrendered.

<84>

21

Rommel and Caligari meet a final time
in the deep dream bunker,
in the coiled recesses of the Fatherland's gut.
And together they open the book of lies and crimes.
Caligari gobbles pig's feet and mystery pills.
He exudes foul vapors.
He belches, he drools and shakes like a syphilitic
and tells Rommel his empty plans tricked out
with the names of gods and ancient heroes.
The Siegfried line, Nibelungen,
Florian Geyer, and Barbarossa,
who will wake from his thousand year sleep
and restore the Reich to glory.
Caligari sits in a corner of his stinking hole
and drivels on about secret weapons:
V-Rocket, U-Boat, A-Bomb, ME-262,
a legion of Aryan sleepwalkers, undead S.S. *Übermenschen*
shot full of Butenandt's latest hormonal extracts.

Caligari is no longer the god of rage,
but a one-eyed palsied man-hag
telling idiot tales by the guttering hearth.
No more bright silver skulls or swastikas.
No Iron Crosses or art deco eagles.
No Valhalla spear carved with runes of power
and secret treaties.

Rommel at last forgets his long forgetting,
knows again what he always knew,
sees lies for lies,
and climbs back to daylight.
On the surface of the earth again, Rommel strips
himself naked, showing his wounds to the sky
and prepares to die.

<85>

22

Two generals in full regalia come for him
bearing a vial: lethal extractive so new
it has no name.
Likewise, his assassins are nameless,
a pair of nonentities carrying one
measured dose of death.
There is no other way, they assure him.
He can not stand trial.
He will not face his faceless accusers.
The generals assure him the poison
will take only a moment to act.
Even this is a lie.

At the funeral, the S.S. honor guard band plays
"Ich hatt' einen Kameraden."
The old Wandervogel song —
sentimental bombast.
Huge black sunwheels loom behind.
A soldier holds Rommel's medals and decorations
on a velvet cushion while von Rundstedt
intones the funeral oration.
The old man speaks as a trance medium,
the voice coming hoarse and hollow
from the farthest, foulest nether-regions,
the bottommost Nibelungen mineshaft.
It echoes up through the cracks and caves,
the last lies Caligari will ever proclaim:
>He was a true son of the Fatherland —
>of blood, honor, and earth.
>He gave his life in true sacrifice —
>for his leader, glory and new birth.

<86>

23

From the far south and east
blows the exhausted breath of Egypt,
what remains of the Khamsin wind
carrying another voice:
the Thrice-Great Hermes speaking from his tomb
which is made entirely of words.
The voice which Rommel heard in the red dust
of el Alamein, in the dust of death.

<87>

The murmurs of the Hermetical books
transformed into pure breath, pure truth.
    You must be born again as a god
    You must be born again
    You must be
    a god.

<88>

PART III:

HONEY FOR THE GODS

1

America, Egypt,
and America again.
The Western Lands.
The abode of the dead.

Air machines drift westward
casting sleek shadows
on the Sphinx, each shadow-shape
a ghostly knife-edge
slicing the stone.

The blood of the Sphinx
comes in hot golden pulses
from the invisible wounds,
not crimson man-blood
but a distilled solar ooze.
Ancient gleaming ichor pours forth
and the sunbaked sand drinks up
every brilliant drop.

<91>

2

He listened to the radio all that day
brain full of truckstop speed and endless miles,
hearing the announcer tell how many times around the
world
you'd have to travel to equal the distance
Apollo had gone on his mission.
A coil wound round the earth
unraveled and stretched from here to the moon.

Fifty weeks traveling per year
and little white pills
and the song on the radio, Led Zeppelin's
"Dazed and Confused," take him there.
Listening to the NASA men and astronauts
making small talk —
the squawk and squelch of outer space CB chatter.
"Breaker, breaker
you got your ears on?"

July 20, 1969, at 10:56 Eastern Daylight Time
Apollo climbed down the ladder
and stepped onto the moon
just as Albion climbed down from the cab,
three metal steps, and put his foot
on the dirt of the breakdown lane
in some desert nowhere.
All around him the dead horizon —
flatness, so much absolute nothing.
So full of white crosses and road rhythm
he'd be able to drive
across the ocean,
around and around the globe
winding his pathway, a bright white string
around the spool of the world.

<92>

And at the perfect moment
he would cast off —
release the string like a fisherman's reel -
and fling himself up there to the moon
which he'd seen rise two hours earlier,
rise like a whale's eye
opening, vast and implacable,
opening in the depths of above.

Too much good German speed,
German diesel and distance,
drives away the dream-state.
After three days up straight
he could hardly remember what sleep was like.
And he got down from his cab,
stood on the roadside
and saw them, actually saw them
— two astronauts and the LEM —
on the moon, like a fleck of dirt on a lens,
a mote in the whale-god's eye.
All around him the flatness
that goes on forever.
"Magnificent desolation." Buzz Aldrin's words
for what he saw on the moon.
But no one understands real desolation
until he's driven round the world
thousands of times and gotten nowhere
and then seen that dead, white behemoth eye
rising over Deseret.

<93>

At a bar at the next crossroads
just over the nameless state line,
he pulled up his rig and went inside
to watch the landing on TV.
So much drunken noise
he could hear nothing
from Houston
just see the crowd of NASA men in white
shirts and black ties, brushcuts like him,
watching a TV screen just like him.
Black and white specters on the moon.

After the first lurching steps
like a baby learning to walk,
Apollo starts hopping.
Inhuman motion —
hopping, like a rabbit,
and then closer to the lens
disappears again.
A silvery gray ghost
which fades, then dissolves
as he approaches the camera,
leached of substance
as he was leached of weight.
A billion viewers watching
all around the world
sucking away Apollo's solidity.

In that nowhere bar, Albion drank nothing
that un-night that never ended,
just dug in his pocket
for another hit of amphetamine
popped it, sucked up some dusty spit
and pulled the pill down his throat.

<94>

3

Left arm sunburnt, permanent squint,
long hair straggling from beneath
a Stetson hat
and a rifle under the seat.
Hands cramping, back hurting,
bladder aching, though it's empty.
Vision blurs and memory curves back on itself.
He's the last cowboy in America
not driving cattle for slaughter
but bees for fertility,
a swirling reproductive swarm
in the trailer.
He is Albion Smith
following the exact path his brother took
fleeing from the High Holy Hill
through Ohio, Illinois martyr-zone,
then catching the path the remnant saints took
all the way across the great American desert
to the Salt Lake.

Eighteen wheeler transporting a million bees
west across America.
A heavy holy fug of hormones
floats behind: honey and nectar,
the wicked sex sugar that
drives all the wild bees,
and all the human creatures he passes by,
mad with desire.
An invisible cloud of pheromones
and a visible trailing cloud of
sex-mad insects
trying to reach and penetrate the rumbling truck vault
where the essence is stored.

<95>

Salt and honey
stinger and cunny
preserve the meat
and make it sweet.

Albion Smith
behind the wheel of a diesel truck
fleeing to the west
fleeing the land of destruction
as Lot fled from blasted Sodom.
Except there is no wife for Albion
and no pillar of salt.
"Let others drink their Mormon tea.
It's German speed that works for me."

Ten gears in forward and five in reverse
hauling the truth, a truck full of bees
and crazed gnosis,
hauling it zigzag across America,
traveling the secret highways of the hive mind.

<96>

4

Over the skies of America
the great shadow squadrons glide.
Over the Washington obelisk
and Alexandria across the Potomac.
Over Cleopatra's needle in Manhattan,
Cairo in Ohio, Memphis,
and the town of Egypt, in York State,
only ten miles down the road
from the Holy Hill of the Mormons.
Teutonic machines of war
float above America,
defying the laws of earth and sky.
They come singing their sad songs of conquest —
losing the war, but winning the battle
for the hearts and minds of their erstwhile enemies.
Over the western continent, America
— the abode of the dead —
come Zeppelins, Heinkel 111 bombers,
Messerschmidt 262s, and the sleek specter
of the perfected V-rocket.

Over the eastern cities
the Appalachian chain
the Mississippi and the plains
the Rockies and the great Salt Lake
over the entire continent
the Teutonic sky-machines float
in their cloud of song,
following the salt axis
east to west:

<97>

the invisible vector
below the skin of the earth.
Go west, Dead Man, go west.
And find your home
among the ancestors
among the gods.

<98>

5

It wasn't the Germans, first.
Von Braun, Dornberger,
their secret rocket-works
at Peenemünde.
It wasn't the Americans
with their captured technology
at the close of the war,
endless freight trains full of V-2s
heading west.
It wasn't the Russians
with Sputnik and space dogs
— Laika, Belka and Strelka —
who first aimed beyond the planet.

It takes an ancient nation
a people, a priestcraft
that knows death and resurrection,
to travel beyond the pull of earth.
It takes true religion and arcane science
— a longing for the sky of souls —
to escape gravity.

The pyramids were built for
Pharaonic soul-flight:
platforms to aim the souls
outward, shooting the spirits
back to the stars.

<99>

All technologies of sky movement
are for soul travel.
All creations of human flight
 — balloon, airplane, zeppelin, ram-jet, V-Rocket -
are technologies for reaching, meeting
and penetrating the realms of the soul.

Movement through three dimensions
is always ritual.
A line is an infinite string of points.
A plane is an infinite progression of lines.
And space is an infinite growth of planes.
A body passing through space
creates the world.
A spirit, a soul-bullet passing through
the upper and outer realms,
creates the universe.

<100>

6

Rommel opens his eyes, rubs away the grit
coughs Sahara dust into the American air.
He spits out the poison that killed him
like a cobra spitting to blind its victim.

Rommel stands at the side of a highway.
It's midnight and a huge truck pulls up,
waits there heaving, panting, shaking,
with a cloud of bees swarming behind.

Rommel sees the cab window roll down.
The driver, in a cowboy hat, leans out
and asks, "How far you going, brother?"
"All the way to the end," Rommel says.

<101>

7

German pharmacology,
German physics, chemistry, engineering,
the most German of engines: Diesel,
German rocket motors and guidance systems,
German rational thought — all of these
flourished under the sign of the sunwheel cross.

Mathematics multiplies
and calculus colonizes the pure
empty sunlit space.
German formulae thrive in the desert,
on the flat plains of reason
under the vast hot eye of day.

But the sun, King Ra himself,
is helpless half of his life.
Proud and imperious,
relentless, unrivaled by day.
Then prisoner of the night sea.

The books of reason dissolve
in the black deeps.
Logic turns to shadow and drifts away,
arithmetic smears, sliding off the page,
molecules go mad and eat themselves
like berserker sharks,
geometry twists and implodes.

<102>

German science fights against this chaos —
the ocean bottomless, endless,
dream-beds and sea caves for the sleepers,
where drowned sailors still roam
full of lust and hunger, thirst and desire,
where lovers, and the dead, are gathered
in shadowy salt-water armies.
Time melts and space flows,
lightning flashes in the deeps,
slow and translucent as a jellyfish.

<103>

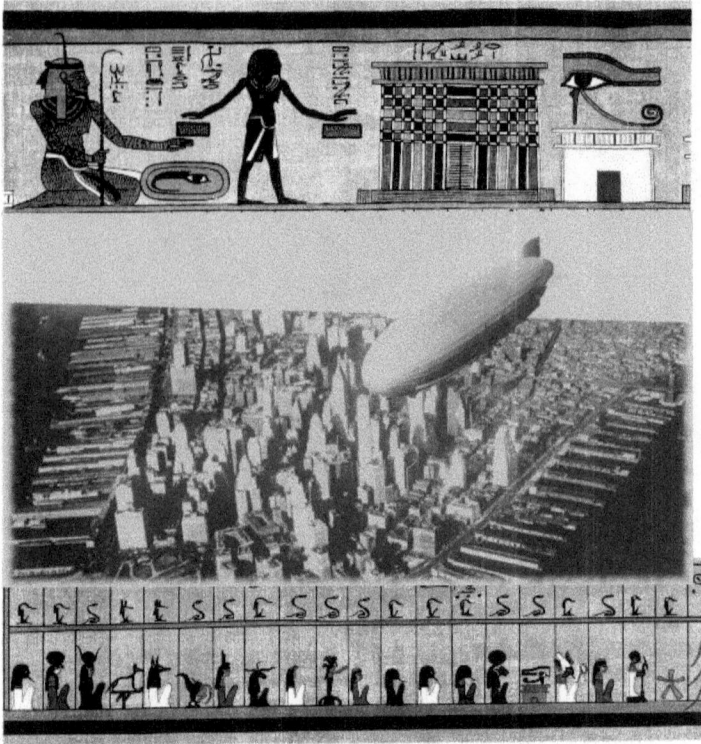

Zeppelins over America
gliding serenely in the dark of the moon,
searchlights scissoring at the sky.
In their radiance, the airships
sail through, indifferent to the
flashes of antiaircraft batteries below,
shrapnel bursting all around.

The zeppelin carries King Ra, the sun,
back to his starting point.
Every night
he returns through occultation to morning,

<104>

two million cubic feet of hydrogen,
solar-gas, Golden Dawn
whaleshape full of unstruck fire,
nascent sun-load
stored in vast hive cells,
the rigid framework of aluminum ribs.

An eighth of a mile long, with
six Maybach diesels to push the vast lozenge of fire
and its payload, baby bombs stored carefully
inside the vast bomb:
    4 pearshaped 660 pounders.
    40 more, a quarter that weight.
    60 fire buckets, each one 25 pounds
    of thermite wrapped in tarred rope.

<105>

Some nights the Americans catch the airships
in their searchlight pincers
and drive them back to sea
where an airborne Viking funeral erupts
burning the ship full of heroes
burning the sky. From fifty miles away
their comrades can see the vast explosion of ur-gas:
night sea journey and morning sky fire.

<106>

On maps, which are always true,
on the secret maps of the northern vastness,
there is a raw red line around the polar lands.
On the far side waits wild-bearded Wotan
with a bomb-bay full of annihilation.
Nordic sorcery, throbbing hoard of atomic death.
But America has the DEW line to keep itself safe.
Twenty-four hours a day, year in and year out,
Distant Early Warning
scanning the northern skies
for incoming attack.

In the far frozen empty places
radar dishes turn slowly,
aiming their invisible probe rays toward the north
whence death must and will come.
Huge ice-crusted saucers tipped on their sides
with quaking zigzagging beams
shooting invisible frequencies into the night sky.

What is beyond the pole?
What desires, so passionately,
America's fiery death?
Bombers, missiles, fighter planes,
the winged messengers of doom,
Lapland witches, rime giants,
great scaly flying worms waiting
for the right moment to rush
in flocks across the white wasteland.

<107>

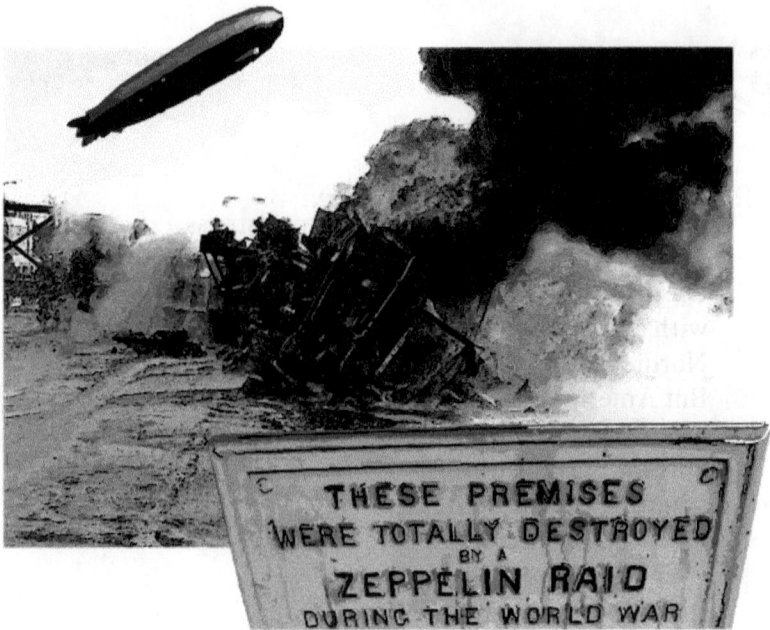

THESE PREMISES
WERE TOTALLY DESTROYED BY A
ZEPPELIN RAID
DURING THE WORLD WAR

Every night
Wotan sends his two ravens, Hugin and Mugin
— Thought and Memory —
to fly out over the world
and bring him back the news.

America has the DEW line
and the vast faceless empire of NORAD —
the North American Air Defense System.
And 40,000 volunteer spotters too,
watchers of the sky, by day, by night,
chanting the ancient hymn.

<108>

He comes, he comes to judge the world
aloud the archangel cries.
While thunders roll from pole to pole
and lightnings cleave the skies.
The afrighted nations hear the sound
and upward lift their eyes.
The slumbering tenants of the ground
in living armies rise.

They come, they come —
the gods are already burning.
Their fiery hair and their brilliant faces,
their armor and their spears
their teeth and their eyes,
the flame that is already sweeping the sky.
They come winging in silver witchshapes
over the pole, the magnetic fields,
arctic wastelands, over the vastness of Canada,
to give the gift of Götterdämmerung:
twilight of the gods
and man.

<109>

10

"Look," Albion says, facing to the north.
"I see them every night. The sky ships."
Rommel turns. He raises his binoculars
and his eyes follow the pointing finger.

Nothing is sleeker, nothing more sinuous
than a Viking dragonship. Serpent's head,
curving neck, glowing eyes, moaning sails,
hiss of the prow cutting the dusk-lit sky.

No vessel richer with occult power
than a U-boat, the longship reborn
beneath the waves. No name on the prow,
only the letter U and three cold digits.

<110>

Black prong, congealed shadows,
snaky-slender, full of night-grace,
the U-boat glides above, disappears,
moves from one dimension to another.

It breaks the plane of the 2-D world
and goes into 3-D or even a fourth,
off the grid of Euclidean space,
up and down, in and out, vanishing.

Viking crew: rime-caked bearded giants.
U-boat crew: squat bearded hunchbacks,
another species of mermen breathing diesel
fumes, ozone, sweat, hormones, brine-vapor.

"The sky ships. I see them every night."
Albion nods to the north. "Out there."
Rommel climbs into the truck's cabin.
"We go west. No? All the way there."

<111>

11

Rumors say that Apollo's moonlandings
were faked. Late night radio stations whisper
as Rommel and Albion head west
in the shadow of the zeppelins.
Nameless announcers claim
the moon shot, the money shot,
was shot in a movie studio.
The Lunar Excursion Module
hadn't really rolled around the moon,
but traveled
like the Manson Dune Buggy death squads
in the deserts of Utah.

However, Rommel and Albion
know the truth.
The astronauts weren't bad actors
in a bad movie.
It's just that NASA landed
on the wrong moon.

All that equipment, rockets,
spacemen dressed
in tinfoil suits and fishbowl helmets,
LEM and orbiter, all those
flight control engineers in Houston
and trouble shooters at Cape Canaveral,
radar displays, glowing altars
in the big, bright TV temple
at Mission Control
to watch the specters, the blips,
ghosts of orbits past and future,

<112>

all those Mormon technocrats
in their white shirts and crewcuts
in their shiny black shoes and skinny ties,
fierce and eager, full of patriotism,
the priests huddled before the green glowing
abode of spirits.

All of this did indeed
take Apollo there —
to the moon.
But it was the wrong *there*.

What did he find?
Dead rock and magnificent desolation.
To reach the moon with rational science
it must be solid and rational itself,
controlled by Germanic physics.
It must be predictable as death,
there exactly when the scientists
think it should be.

Thirty billion dollars,
ten years of frenzied work, incinerated astronauts,
a sky full of silvery cinders.
And what did Apollo do on this moon?
Fly the stiff aluminum flag
in the airless windless place of conquest.
Play a little golf in the bright
infertile lunar desert.
And drive around like a drunken frat boy.
And bring back some rocks.

<113>

12

"This is the spot," Albion says,
on the far side of the Mississippi,
"where they hid Joseph's body."
Lynch mob murder. Secret burial.

Picks and shovels in blue midnight.
"The Elders dug him up, when they
knew it was time to go west again."
All the way to the Rocky Mountains.

To the Great Salt Basin, where
an ocean of tears crystallized
into America's own Dead Sea,
lake of a billion secret griefs.

"They took him in a Conestoga
with the two mummies he bought
from a traveling Ohio mountebank
in the wagon-hearse of the elect."

In a cask of honey, sterile and pure,
carried west like great Lord Nelson
after death at the Battle of Trafalgar,
in a tun of bee's sweetness, gold elixir.

"He said honey is the blood of the gods
oozing free in sunlight from the combs.
He told the saints to store him up after
his death in a barrel of the sun's nectar."

<114>

13

At death, each Latter Day Saint
is raised to divinity.
At death, each Man-Mormon
is raised to Apollo's throne.
A god, not just of a planet,
but his own solar system.

Every Mormon Heaven
can be reached by spaceship —
a literal, physical, actual place.
For the Prophet: the Kolob galaxy
where the god of planet Earth rules.
For it is written:
"As man now is
God once was."

Gold is the sun's metal and essence.
The prophet found golden plates
and made a golden Bible.
A gold angel stands guard
on the Obelisk, high Egyptian overlord
at Hill Cumorah.
American Apollo, god of the sun.

<115>

14

A golden angel stands too
atop the temple
in Salt Lake City.
But its glory is just for tourists
and the uninitiated.

The real Holy of Holies
is twenty miles south east of there —
the vast Bunker of the Dead
at Granite Mountain, dug
into the living rock
and laid out exactly
as the interior chambers
of the Great Pyramid at Giza.
Four billion names
and thousands more every day
stored there on microfilm and digital arcana.

Names of the endless dead
preserved, organized, and given
spiritual rebirth in proxy marriage —
secret ceremonies of endowment.
Everyone who ever lived, and for whom
there's some written record,
will eventually be captured
and stored in the Vault of Names.
Married in ghost-weddings
to make a vast interstellar hive
of future divinities
spreading outward
across the universe.

<116>

Steel doors strong enough to withstand
a nuclear blast, acres of underground
filing systems. Fallout shelter of the dead.
Saving the ancestors from oblivion.

And secret safety chambers where the elders
can wait out the radioactive storm
with freeze-dried food
to last a hundred years, a groundwater
purification system,
stocks of morphine and amphetamine,
the Golden Bible itself,
and room for ten young wives each,
for select church leaders.
And frozen sperm
if the elders prove too eldritch
to reproduce in their Fortress of Fertility.
Seed and names
claimed and reclaimed.
Names and seed
thus is it decreed.

<117>

15

And the sacred barrel —
more precious than the golden plates
themselves, or the magic peepstone,
or the Urim and Thummim.
The secret bee-slime casket
where Joseph the Prophet's body
has hunched, hidden, since the night
the brave gravebreakers found him
and freed him from the cold earth.
A cooper's crude construction:
oaken staves, hand-shaved,
three rusty iron hoops,
the whole cask daubed
with hieroglyphics:
Eye of Horus
Tau cross
Scarab
Ankh.

Too fragile to be opened,
now it rests on the high altar,
sealed tight in sheathes of thermoplastic.
X-rays fifty years back
revealed that the Prophet was indeed
in there, intact,
folded in a larval crouch,
head titled back
mouth opened wide
as though shouting
at the sky,
shouting
all the way to Kolob.

<118>

A king bee, unborn
in his Canopic hive-cell
in ancient Royal Priesthood Jelly —
human yolk in honey plasm
waiting to hatch
and rise
as a god.

<119>

16

Rommel and Albion take turns driving,
crossing the moon-baked western lands.
Rommel, knowing panzer and half-track,
grips the wheel and works the shifter.

He knows the grind of fouled gears,
the clatter of well-maintained diesel,
the stink of exhaust, burnt motor oil
and coolant boiling from the radiator.

Far across the desert, in the sunset,
he sees the ghosts of German V-2s
transformed into Redstone rockets,
taking off from secret testing range.

A dune-buggy, racing itself off road,
off the map, zaps in deadly rhythm
like a buzz-bomb homing its target,
kicking up pale plumes of night dust.

Sleepless. No need any more for sleep.
Dry-mouthed. No need for any water.
Rommel hasn't eaten since El Alamein
or heard a single syllable auf Deutsch.

"Tomorrow," Albion says, sitting up.
"Tomorrow we make it to Salt Lake."
He nods, blinks back the phantoms
and spits out his saliva-sucking stone.

<120>

17

The last zeppelin holds the hydrogen
sun, in occultation.
The last zeppelin
drifts from east to west,
flying only in the dark of the moon —
the last three days of the lunar cycle.
The night sky: where true desire
can not be be repressed.

The last Jesus holds the hydrocarbon
moon, in occultation.
The last, whitest Jesus in the world,
with his long locks of honey-gold hair,
sensitive lips and the perfect complexion
any teenaged girl would envy.
Sun-washed daylight savior
emerges after three days in the tomb
of his ancestors.
The day sky: where true desire
can not be manifested.

Rommel to Albion:
"This is as far as we can go
using reason.
Beyond this point, we must
employ unreason."
Did he speak in German, or English?
Did he speak at all?

<121>

18

Wotan, War Father
the crimson saint,
specter of unreason
emerges at solstice.
He flies into the icy night sky
roaring in black vacuum,
in the dark of the moon,
leaving contrails of iridescent frost spume,
two bright scars in the skin of night.
He rides with his bag of joy-toys:
moonrocks and magic animals
stinking herbs, ice-dolls
and a handful of quicksilver,
essence of the moon
bright and quivering
oozing between his fingers.

Nordic saint, pagan master, and monster.
Divine portent, sacred omen.
Frankenstein's North Pole creature
cobbled together from body parts
and gothic desire,
the blood of sacrificial horses,
fragments of superstition and bone,
unforgotten folk magic
and the hallucinogenic blur
of Arctic mushrooms.

A jolly old man with a beard and a whip
and a string of frozen drool hanging from his lip.
In the shape of a man, but gigantic in stature,
with long locks of ragged hair,
reaching out his vast hand
the color and texture of a mummy.

<122>

19

Gravity, the god of science,
the force of reason
holding together the cosmos,
grabs Wotan's sky-sledge,
pulls it close, making one golden ring
around the world.
One wreath of cold midnight light
and its slow-dying remnant.
One electron ring
around the nucleus —
Earth.
Making it
one atom.
Hydrogen.

<123>

20

Rommel and Albion, Egypt in America,
come through the final pass and see
the Mormon pyramid raised by God
himself, Granite Mountain of souls.

The end-time cavern, spiritual fallout
shelter with four arched entry holes,
repository bank vault carved straight
into the raw rock desert valley wall.

And see the first and last Teutonic
bomb-ship, the War Father's zeppelin,
riding at sky-anchor above the highest,
holiest, safest, most secret of mountains.

A moonless night, a last night on earth.
Beyond: no days, no centuries, no time.
Pure entropic nothingness, time itself
pulverized, ground into hydrogen atoms.

Rommel nods and says, "This is true:
zeppelins and honey bees are unable
to fly. It goes against rational sense,
gravitational physics, all our theory."

A vast hovering hive, separated into
octagon cells, swollen hydrogen bags
and nectar sacs. "They modeled the
zeppelin on the honey bee. It's true."

<124>

The hum of diesel, the buzz of wings.
Then they see it: the zeppelin opens
its belly, disgorging. The sweet fiery
load descends in a blinding downpour.

Albion gets out, swings open the truck's
rear doors. And with one bang of the fist
he sends his million bees outward to join
the firestorm, the soul swarm, above.

<125>

21

The last midnight:
the night of nights
when truth comes in
torrents of heavenfire.
No ice. No snow. No ragged shepherds.
No gifts. No astrologers from the east.
Only two dead men and a truckload of bees
rising.
No angelic hordes, rapturous in song.
No star in the east,
but writhing sky-snakes —
battle-maidens screaming in dread ecstasy
as they plummet one last time from Valhalla.
The silent roar of the aurora borealis —
the northern incendiary rain
drenching the desert.
And four billion souls awake.

Magnetic North Pole pulls
every compass needle straight up,
just as the War Father comes
to wrench the dead from the ground,
just as a magnet boom-crane
in the endless junkyard of souls
pulls wrecks from the wreckage.
The minute hand and the hour hand
stand straight up rigid
because it's always midnight at the North Pole
and it's always midnight when he returns.

<126>

The Latter Day Saints had planned
for H-bomb hammer blows.
The elders had expected thermonuclear
knock-knock-knocking on their four secret doors.
Not the suction vortex of Valkyrie fire storm.
They'd planned to keep invaders out,
not to keep captive souls in.

So the prison explodes,
the blast-doors blast open:
one two three and four.
And four billion names, souls, voices,
come pouring out of the four tunnel holes,
braiding themselves into four luminous rivers
into the swarm of swarms.

A fifth,
buzzing, yearning, burning,
joins the god-coil,
golden bright, swirling upward
with smoke and ozone,
negative air pressure and X-ray blur.
Thunderous shouts
of four billions souls
now one.

The barrel is the last to explode,
deep inside the cave.
The last American Pharaoh, freed
from his followers
and his Canopic ooze-bed.

<127>

The bomb at the heart of the tomb
shoots the prophet's remains
from the heaving honey-womb,
shoots him, white shrapnel,
secret weapon of the dead —
ribs, femurs, skull, tibia
clattering jawbone —
straight to Kolob.

<128>

22

The god-coil
— the rising radiation swarm —
reaches, writhing
into the heaven-heavy sky.
The Visible God — countless larva hatching,
seething white pulse in blackness
red-webbed with blood threads
mad with honey-hunger, sex hormones,
insect speed — the last God
glows and pours upward,
outward.

In the desert below,
spent amphetamine shells
and grave rhymes
talk to themselves
with idiot intensity.
"Bees can't fly."
"Souls can't die."
"Stars can't cry."
"Words can't lie."

White crosses in the crust of the earth.
Two scarabs scuttling under the crushed
burnt-out husk of a tractor trailer.
Two empty skulls shaking in the dirt.

<129>

"Listen," one skull hisses. "Listen!
Hydrogen and gravity make a star.
Hydrogen and gravity and that's all."

"I hear," the other one says. "I hear."

And hears
silence.

<130>

THE BURNT-OVER DISTRICT

Western York State — where I've lived my entire life — was called The Burnt-Over District for all the souls who caught fire here, sparked and breathed into flames by preachers and prophets passing through. But why such dread revelation in this particular hinterland? Why in this place, two hundred miles from end to end, with the Grand Erie Canal as the spine, why here in this slice of forgotten backwater nowhere did the gods, did God himself, and Satan, God's Ape, range so freely?

It was from the beginning a place of spiritual madness: ghost-talkers, prophets, preachers, small time saviors, devil-drivers, founders of cults and world religions. It was a place of mad spirit: revelation, golden Bibles and midnight black, chiliasm, magic amulets, sanctity, sin and secret holy war.

Lorenzo "Crazy" Dow passed through here repeatedly, incognito mostly, under cover of night. Filthy, bearded, black-caped, he appeared and disappeared unbidden.

Charles Grandison Finney descended from the frozen North Country like a fiery whirlwind. Tall and thin as a whip, with eyes described by one convert as having "uncanny hypnotic power," he forced sinners to fall weeping before him, begging for mercy.

Jemima Wilkinson was killed by God, brought back to life as the Publick and Universal Friend, and established her 12,000-acre New Jerusalem in the Finger Lakes.

Father Nash prayed so loudly that his pious shouts could be heard a mile away, more terrible than the battle-cries of savage warriors.

John Humphrey Noyes took unto himself multiple wives and taught the secrets of "male continence" to his followers.

God, or the blessed dead, spoke through the mouths of two teenaged girls, those fetching Fox sisters of Hydesville.

Mordechai Noah bought a piece of Grand Island just above Niagara Falls, to create his "Ararat, a city of Refuge for the Jews."

And Joseph Smith, Holy Joe, The Prophet, "author and proprietor" of *The Book of Mormon*, got his start here too.

They were a strange tribe, these sanctified solitaries, chasing both Satan and God across York state. Full of pagan sound and Christian fury, givers and defenders of the law, and yet lawbreakers

<131>

one and all. Some battled the temporal arm; others fought a more spiritualized battle. Noyes waged a decades-long war with the local authorities, accused of bigamy and preying on innocent young girls. Dow and Finney met the enemy hand to hand and man to man, shouting him down from the pulpit and stump. Like the boxer in the ring, though surrounded by a thousand screaming witnesses, all of these holy warriors were ultimately alone with their opponents.

Dow, Fox, Finney, Wilkinson, Nash, Noyes and Noah — the names are largely forgotten now. But one — Smith — is still well remembered, much beloved, venerated as God's greatest revelator.

Proximity is power. And I'm downwind. It's only twenty miles to the place where Mormonism began, where the fastest-growing, the richest, the whitest and weirdest religion in America got its start. The easiest way to make sense of my fascination with arcane mormonistica is to look at a map. The Wayne County line is only ten miles from my house. The High Holy Mormon sites (Palmyra, the Hill Cumorah, the sacred grove) are just another ten miles beyond that.

And I'm downwind. Picture a religious Chernobyl, spiritual radioactivity rising over the meltdown and then drifting westward toward me. A steady — if barely-noticeable — dusting of religious fallout might indeed have coated my entire life. Or perhaps a volcano is a better image: magma boiling from the top of Hill Cumorah where the angel Moroni statue stands, sending up a cloud of smoke and ash that floats toward Rochester, not exactly blotting out the sun, but giving this place some of its baleful gray gloom.

It is still a strange place, a very strange place. Between 1790 and 1850, this wide strip of land that parallels blue Ontario's south shore was the overfertile hotbed for more religious power than any region on earth. Something strange and terrible happened here. A Spirit, or spirits, moved and the land itself still retains the memory.

<132>

ABOUT THIS BOOK

The body type for this book is Aldine, a typeface based on originals by Aldus Manutius, the great Venetian humanist printer and publisher. Section titles are set in Decorated 035 and numerals for the poems are set in Vineta, two typefaces suggesting the "Egyptian" style of lettering made popular after the French Empire's first wave of Egyptomania. Showcard Gothic and Goudy Heavface, faces suggesting the silent-film era of *The Cabinet of Dr. Caligari*, are featured on the title-page.

The illustrations for this book are by Brett Rutherford, digital montage art assembled from numerous sources: The Budge edition of *The Egyptian Book of the Dead*; several Mormon histories; public domain news archive images, stills from *The Cabinet of Dr. Caligari*, and digital collages of various photos. The Bayer logo is from the pharmaceutical manufacturer's headquarters building in Munich. The illustrations are printed in grayscale in the print edition, but are in full color in the ebook version. Some of the montages involve as many as three levels of myth, such as the four-baboon image representing Thoth from the *Egyptian Book of the Dead*, overlaid with a stone sigil carved by Joseph Smith, and that in turn overlaid with the Nazi swastika.

<133>